50 Classic Italian Pasta Recipes

By: Kelly Johnson

Table of Contents

- Spaghetti alla Carbonara
- Fettuccine Alfredo
- Penne all'Arrabbiata
- Linguine alle Vongole
- Bucatini all'Amatriciana
- Spaghetti al Pomodoro
- Tagliatelle al Ragù Bolognese
- Pappardelle ai Funghi Porcini
- Orecchiette con Cime di Rapa
- Rigatoni alla Norma
- Lasagna alla Bolognese
- Cannelloni Ripieni
- Fusilli al Pesto Genovese
- Ravioli di Ricotta e Spinaci
- Tortellini in Brodo
- Gnocchi alla Sorrentina
- Spaghetti Aglio e Olio
- Penne alla Vodka
- Linguine al Nero di Seppia
- Pici cacio e pepe
- Fettuccine ai Frutti di Mare
- Paccheri al Forno
- Cappelletti in Brodo
- Rigatoni con Salsiccia e Funghi
- Tagliolini al Tartufo
- Vermicelli alla Puttanesca
- Spaghetti alla Chitarra
- Farfalle al Salmone
- Lasagna di Verdure
- Fusilli con Gorgonzola e Noci
- Conchiglie al Formaggio
- Trofie al Pesto di Pistacchio
- Tagliatelle ai Carciofi
- Pappardelle al Cinghiale
- Penne Zucchine e Gamberetti

- Gnocchi di Patate al Tartufo
- Pasta alla Genovese
- Spaghetti alla Marinara
- Linguine alle Cozze
- Maccheroni al Forno
- Penne alla Crudaiola
- Fusilli al Tonno
- Paccheri con Melanzane e Ricotta
- Pici all'Aglione
- Tortelloni di Zucca
- Strozzapreti al Ragù di Coniglio
- Orecchiette al Pomodoro e Basilico
- Fregola con Vongole
- Ravioli al Tartufo
- Spaghetti con Bottarga

Spaghetti alla Carbonara

Ingredients:

- 400g (14 oz) spaghetti
- 100g (3.5 oz) pancetta or guanciale, diced
- 2 large eggs
- 1 large egg yolk
- 50g (1.8 oz) Pecorino Romano cheese, grated
- 50g (1.8 oz) Parmesan cheese, grated
- Freshly ground black pepper
- Salt (for pasta water)
- 2 tbsp olive oil (optional, for frying pancetta)

Instructions:

1. **Cook the Spaghetti:**
    - Bring a large pot of salted water to a boil.
    - Cook the spaghetti until al dente according to the package instructions.
2. **Prepare the Pancetta:**
    - While the pasta cooks, heat a large frying pan over medium heat.
    - Add the diced pancetta (and olive oil, if using) and cook until it's crispy and golden. Remove from heat and set aside.
3. **Make the Sauce:**
    - In a bowl, whisk together the eggs, egg yolk, Pecorino Romano, and Parmesan cheese. Add a generous amount of freshly ground black pepper.
4. **Combine Everything:**
    - Reserve about 1 cup of pasta water before draining the spaghetti.
    - Drain the spaghetti and immediately transfer it to the pan with the pancetta.
    - Toss to combine and let the heat from the pasta slightly cook the pancetta further.
    - Remove the pan from the heat and quickly pour in the egg and cheese mixture, stirring constantly to create a creamy sauce. Add a little reserved pasta water if the sauce is too thick.
5. **Serve:**

    - Plate the pasta and serve with extra grated cheese and a sprinkle of black pepper.

Fettuccine Alfredo

Ingredients:

- 400g (14 oz) fettuccine
- 100g (3.5 oz) unsalted butter
- 150g (5.3 oz) Parmesan cheese, grated
- Salt (for pasta water)
- Freshly ground black pepper
- Optional: Heavy cream (for a creamier version)

Instructions:

1. **Cook the Fettuccine**:
   - Bring a large pot of salted water to a boil.
   - Cook the fettuccine until al dente according to the package instructions.
2. **Prepare the Alfredo Sauce**:
   - In a large pan, melt the butter over low heat.
   - Once melted, add a small amount of the pasta water and the grated Parmesan cheese. Stir until a smooth sauce forms. If you prefer a creamier sauce, you can add a splash of heavy cream.
3. **Combine and Serve**:
   - Drain the fettuccine, reserving some pasta water.
   - Add the fettuccine to the pan with the Alfredo sauce, tossing to coat. Add more pasta water if needed to adjust the consistency.
   - Season with freshly ground black pepper and serve immediately.

Penne all'Arrabbiata

Ingredients:

- 400g (14 oz) penne pasta
- 3 tbsp olive oil
- 3 garlic cloves, minced
- 1-2 red chili peppers, chopped (adjust to taste)
- 400g (14 oz) canned tomatoes, crushed
- Salt (for pasta water and sauce)
- Freshly ground black pepper
- Fresh parsley, chopped (for garnish)
- Optional: Grated Parmesan cheese (for serving)

Instructions:

1. **Cook the Penne:**
   - Bring a large pot of salted water to a boil.
   - Cook the penne until al dente according to the package instructions.
2. **Prepare the Arrabbiata Sauce:**
   - Heat the olive oil in a large pan over medium heat.
   - Add the minced garlic and chopped chili peppers, cooking for 1-2 minutes until fragrant.
   - Add the crushed tomatoes, season with salt and black pepper, and simmer for about 10-15 minutes until the sauce thickens.
3. **Combine and Serve:**
   - Drain the penne and add it to the sauce. Toss to coat well.
   - Garnish with fresh parsley and serve with grated Parmesan cheese if desired.

Linguine alle Vongole

Ingredients:

- 400g (14 oz) linguine
- 1kg (2.2 lbs) fresh clams, cleaned
- 4 tbsp olive oil
- 2 garlic cloves, minced
- 1/2 cup dry white wine
- Fresh parsley, chopped
- Salt (for pasta water)
- Freshly ground black pepper
- Red pepper flakes (optional)

Instructions:

1. **Cook the Linguine:**
    - Bring a large pot of salted water to a boil.
    - Cook the linguine until al dente according to the package instructions.
2. **Prepare the Clams:**
    - Heat olive oil in a large pan over medium heat.
    - Add the minced garlic and cook until fragrant.
    - Add the clams and pour in the white wine. Cover and cook for 5-7 minutes, until the clams open. Discard any clams that do not open.
3. **Combine and Serve:**
    - Drain the linguine and add it to the pan with the clams. Toss well to combine.
    - Sprinkle with freshly chopped parsley, black pepper, and red pepper flakes if using.
    - Serve immediately.

Bucatini all'Amatriciana

Ingredients:

- 400g bucatini pasta
- 150g guanciale (pork cheek), diced
- 400g canned peeled tomatoes
- 1 small onion, finely chopped
- 1/2 teaspoon red chili flakes
- 50g Pecorino Romano cheese, grated
- Salt and black pepper to taste

Instructions:

1. Cook the bucatini in salted boiling water until al dente.
2. In a large skillet, cook the guanciale until crispy. Remove and set aside.
3. In the same skillet, sauté the onion until soft. Add the chili flakes.
4. Add the tomatoes and simmer for 15 minutes.
5. Mix the guanciale back in, then toss with the cooked bucatini.
6. Serve topped with Pecorino Romano.

Spaghetti al Pomodoro

Ingredients:

- 400g spaghetti
- 500g fresh tomatoes, blanched and peeled
- 2 garlic cloves, minced
- 4 tablespoons olive oil
- Fresh basil leaves
- Salt and black pepper to taste

Instructions:

1. Cook the spaghetti in salted boiling water until al dente.
2. In a skillet, sauté garlic in olive oil until golden.
3. Add chopped tomatoes, basil, salt, and pepper, then simmer for 20 minutes.
4. Toss the cooked spaghetti with the sauce.
5. Garnish with extra basil before serving.

Tagliatelle al Ragù Bolognese

Ingredients:

- 400g tagliatelle
- 200g ground beef
- 200g ground pork
- 1 carrot, finely chopped
- 1 celery stalk, finely chopped
- 1 onion, finely chopped
- 300ml tomato puree
- 100ml red wine
- 100ml milk
- Olive oil
- Salt and pepper to taste

Instructions:

1. In a large pot, heat oil and sauté carrot, celery, and onion until soft.
2. Add the meats, browning well. Pour in wine and let it evaporate.
3. Stir in tomato puree and simmer for 2 hours, adding milk at the end.
4. Cook the tagliatelle in salted boiling water until al dente.
5. Toss the pasta with the ragù and serve with grated Parmesan.

Pappardelle ai Funghi Porcini

Ingredients:

- 400g pappardelle
- 300g fresh porcini mushrooms, sliced
- 2 garlic cloves, minced
- 3 tablespoons olive oil
- 50ml white wine
- Fresh parsley, chopped
- Salt and pepper to taste

Instructions:

1. Cook the pappardelle in salted boiling water until al dente.
2. In a skillet, heat olive oil and sauté garlic until fragrant.
3. Add mushrooms and cook until they release their moisture.
4. Pour in white wine and let it evaporate.
5. Toss the pasta with the mushrooms, season, and sprinkle with parsley.

Orecchiette con Cime di Rapa

Ingredients:

- 400g orecchiette
- 300g cime di rapa (broccoli rabe), chopped
- 2 garlic cloves, minced
- 2 anchovy fillets
- 3 tablespoons olive oil
- Red chili flakes (optional)
- Salt and pepper to taste

Instructions:

1. Cook the orecchiette in salted boiling water with cime di rapa.
2. In a skillet, heat olive oil, add garlic and anchovies, cooking until fragrant.
3. Toss the drained pasta and greens with the anchovy mixture.
4. Add chili flakes if desired, and serve hot.

Rigatoni alla Norma

Ingredients:

- 400g rigatoni
- 2 large eggplants, diced
- 400g canned peeled tomatoes
- 2 garlic cloves, minced
- Olive oil
- Fresh basil
- 150g ricotta salata, grated
- Salt and pepper to taste

Instructions:

1. Cook the rigatoni in salted boiling water until al dente.
2. Fry eggplant in olive oil until golden, then drain on paper towels.
3. Sauté garlic in a skillet, add tomatoes, and simmer for 15 minutes.
4. Add eggplant to the sauce and toss with cooked rigatoni.
5. Serve with grated ricotta salata and basil.

Lasagna alla Bolognese

Ingredients:

- 500g lasagna sheets
- 500g ragù Bolognese (see recipe above)
- 500ml béchamel sauce
- 150g grated Parmesan cheese

Instructions:

1. Preheat oven to 180°C (350°F).
2. In a baking dish, layer lasagna sheets, ragù, béchamel, and Parmesan.
3. Repeat layers, finishing with béchamel and Parmesan.
4. Bake for 45 minutes until bubbly and golden.

Cannelloni Ripieni

Ingredients:

- 250g cannelloni pasta
- 500g ricotta cheese
- 100g spinach, cooked and chopped
- 1 egg
- 500ml tomato sauce
- 100g grated Parmesan
- Salt, pepper, and nutmeg to taste

Instructions:

1. Preheat oven to 180°C (350°F).
2. Mix ricotta, spinach, egg, and seasonings.
3. Stuff cannelloni with the ricotta mixture.
4. Spread a layer of tomato sauce in a baking dish, arrange cannelloni, cover with remaining sauce, and sprinkle with Parmesan.
5. Bake for 30 minutes.

Fusilli al Pesto Genovese

Ingredients:

- 400g fusilli
- 100g fresh basil leaves
- 50g pine nuts
- 2 garlic cloves
- 100ml olive oil
- 50g grated Parmesan
- Salt to taste

Instructions:

1. Cook the fusilli in salted boiling water until al dente.
2. Blend basil, pine nuts, garlic, and olive oil into a smooth pesto.
3. Stir in Parmesan and season with salt.
4. Toss the cooked fusilli with the pesto and serve.

Ravioli di Ricotta e Spinaci

Ingredients:

- 400g ravioli dough
- 250g ricotta cheese
- 150g spinach, cooked and finely chopped
- 50g grated Parmesan cheese
- Nutmeg, salt, and pepper to taste
- 50g butter
- Fresh sage leaves

Instructions:

1. Combine ricotta, spinach, Parmesan, nutmeg, salt, and pepper for the filling.
2. Roll out the dough and place small mounds of filling at intervals.
3. Cover with another sheet of dough, seal, and cut into ravioli.
4. Cook ravioli in boiling salted water until they float.
5. Melt butter, add sage leaves, and toss ravioli in the sage butter.
6. Serve with additional Parmesan.

Tortellini in Brodo

Ingredients:

- 400g tortellini, preferably with meat filling
- 1.5 liters of chicken or beef broth
- Grated Parmesan cheese for serving

Instructions:

1. Heat the broth until simmering.
2. Cook the tortellini in the broth until they float.
3. Serve hot with grated Parmesan on top.

Gnocchi alla Sorrentina

Ingredients:

- 500g potato gnocchi
- 400g tomato sauce
- 250g mozzarella, diced
- 50g grated Parmesan
- Fresh basil leaves

Instructions:

1. Cook gnocchi in boiling salted water until they float.
2. Toss gnocchi with tomato sauce in an oven-safe dish.
3. Top with mozzarella and Parmesan.
4. Bake at 180°C (350°F) until the cheese is melted and bubbly.
5. Garnish with basil leaves.

Spaghetti Aglio e Olio

Ingredients:

- 400g spaghetti
- 4 garlic cloves, thinly sliced
- 100ml olive oil
- Red chili flakes (optional)
- Fresh parsley, chopped
- Salt to taste

Instructions:

1. Cook spaghetti in salted boiling water until al dente.
2. In a skillet, sauté garlic in olive oil until golden.
3. Add chili flakes, then toss with the drained spaghetti.
4. Sprinkle with parsley and serve.

Penne alla Vodka

Ingredients:

- 400g penne pasta
- 200ml tomato puree
- 100ml heavy cream
- 50ml vodka
- 2 garlic cloves, minced
- 2 tablespoons olive oil
- Grated Parmesan cheese for serving
- Salt and pepper to taste

Instructions:

1. Cook penne in salted boiling water until al dente.
2. In a skillet, sauté garlic in olive oil.
3. Add tomato puree and vodka, simmer until the alcohol evaporates.
4. Stir in cream, salt, and pepper.
5. Toss with cooked penne and serve with Parmesan.

Linguine al Nero di Seppia

Ingredients:

- 400g linguine
- 2-3 squid, cleaned and cut into rings
- 2 garlic cloves, minced
- 1 small onion, finely chopped
- 1 sachet of squid ink
- 100ml white wine
- Olive oil
- Salt and pepper to taste

Instructions:

1. Cook linguine in salted boiling water until al dente.
2. Sauté garlic and onion in olive oil, add squid and cook briefly.
3. Deglaze with white wine, then stir in squid ink.
4. Toss the linguine with the sauce and season to taste.

Pici Cacio e Pepe

Ingredients:

- 400g pici pasta
- 200g Pecorino Romano cheese, grated
- 2 teaspoons black pepper, freshly ground
- Salt to taste

Instructions:

1. Cook pici in salted boiling water until al dente.
2. Toast black pepper in a dry pan.
3. Mix cheese with a bit of pasta water to create a creamy sauce.
4. Toss the cooked pici with the cheese and pepper, adjusting with more pasta water if needed.

Fettuccine ai Frutti di Mare

Ingredients:

- 400g fettuccine
- 300g mixed seafood (shrimp, mussels, clams, squid)
- 3 garlic cloves, minced
- 200ml white wine
- 3 tablespoons olive oil
- Fresh parsley, chopped
- Salt and pepper to taste

Instructions:

1. Cook fettuccine in salted boiling water until al dente.
2. In a skillet, sauté garlic in olive oil, then add seafood.
3. Pour in white wine, cover, and cook until seafood is done.
4. Toss with cooked fettuccine and sprinkle with parsley.

Paccheri al Forno

Ingredients:

- 400g paccheri pasta
- 500ml tomato sauce
- 250g mozzarella, diced
- 150g ricotta cheese
- 100g grated Parmesan
- 2 garlic cloves, minced
- Olive oil
- Fresh basil leaves

Instructions:

1. Cook paccheri in salted boiling water until al dente.
2. Mix tomato sauce, garlic, and a bit of olive oil.
3. Layer paccheri, mozzarella, ricotta, and tomato sauce in a baking dish.
4. Top with Parmesan and bake at 180°C (350°F) until bubbly.
5. Garnish with basil before serving.

Cappelletti in Brodo

Ingredients:

- 400g cappelletti, preferably with meat filling
- 1.5 liters of beef or chicken broth
- Grated Parmesan cheese for serving

Instructions:

1. Heat the broth until simmering.
2. Cook the cappelletti in the broth until they float.
3. Serve hot with grated Parmesan on top.

Rigatoni con Salsiccia e Funghi

Ingredients:

- 400g rigatoni pasta
- 300g Italian sausage, crumbled
- 200g mushrooms, sliced
- 1 onion, chopped
- 2 garlic cloves, minced
- 200ml heavy cream
- Olive oil
- Salt and pepper to taste
- Grated Parmesan for serving

Instructions:

1. Cook rigatoni in salted boiling water until al dente.
2. In a skillet, sauté onion and garlic in olive oil, then add sausage and cook until browned.
3. Add mushrooms and cook until soft.
4. Stir in cream, season with salt and pepper, and toss with rigatoni.
5. Serve with Parmesan.

Tagliolini al Tartufo

Ingredients:

- 400g tagliolini pasta
- 40g black truffle, finely shaved
- 100g butter
- Salt to taste
- Grated Parmesan for serving

Instructions:

1. Cook tagliolini in salted boiling water until al dente.
2. Melt butter in a skillet, add truffle shavings, and gently warm.
3. Toss the tagliolini with the truffle butter and serve with Parmesan.

Vermicelli alla Puttanesca

Ingredients:

- 400g vermicelli pasta
- 400g canned tomatoes, chopped
- 3 garlic cloves, minced
- 50g black olives, sliced
- 30g capers
- 2 anchovy fillets
- 1 chili pepper, chopped
- Olive oil
- Fresh parsley, chopped
- Salt to taste

Instructions:

1. Cook vermicelli in salted boiling water until al dente.
2. In a skillet, sauté garlic, anchovies, and chili in olive oil.
3. Add tomatoes, olives, capers, and cook until sauce thickens.
4. Toss vermicelli with the sauce, sprinkle with parsley, and serve.

Spaghetti alla Chitarra

Ingredients:

- 400g spaghetti alla chitarra pasta
- 300g fresh tomatoes, diced
- 2 garlic cloves, minced
- Olive oil
- Fresh basil leaves
- Salt to taste

Instructions:

1. Cook spaghetti in salted boiling water until al dente.
2. In a skillet, sauté garlic in olive oil, add tomatoes and cook until softened.
3. Toss spaghetti with the tomato sauce, garnish with basil, and serve.

Farfalle al Salmone

Ingredients:

- 400g farfalle pasta
- 200g smoked salmon, sliced
- 200ml heavy cream
- 1 onion, finely chopped
- 2 tablespoons vodka
- Olive oil
- Fresh dill, chopped
- Salt and pepper to taste

Instructions:

1. Cook farfalle in salted boiling water until al dente.
2. Sauté onion in olive oil until soft, add vodka, and let it evaporate.
3. Add cream, salmon, and season with salt and pepper.
4. Toss with farfalle and garnish with dill.

Lasagna di Verdure

Ingredients:

- 12 lasagna sheets
- 400g mixed vegetables (zucchini, eggplant, bell peppers), diced
- 500ml tomato sauce
- 300g ricotta cheese
- 200g mozzarella, diced
- 50g grated Parmesan
- Olive oil
- Salt and pepper to taste

Instructions:

1. Sauté vegetables in olive oil, season with salt and pepper.
2. Layer lasagna sheets, ricotta, vegetables, and tomato sauce in a baking dish.
3. Top with mozzarella and Parmesan.
4. Bake at 180°C (350°F) until bubbly.

Fusilli con Gorgonzola e Noci

Ingredients:

- 400g fusilli pasta
- 200g Gorgonzola cheese
- 100g walnuts, chopped
- 200ml heavy cream
- Salt and pepper to taste
- Fresh parsley, chopped

Instructions:

1. Cook fusilli in salted boiling water until al dente.
2. Melt Gorgonzola in a saucepan with cream, then stir in walnuts.
3. Toss with fusilli, season with salt and pepper, and garnish with parsley.

Conchiglie al Formaggio

Ingredients:

- 400g conchiglie (shell pasta)
- 200g mixed cheese (cheddar, Parmesan, mozzarella), grated
- 200ml milk
- 2 tablespoons butter
- 2 tablespoons flour
- Salt and pepper to taste

Instructions:

1. Cook conchiglie in salted boiling water until al dente.
2. Make a roux with butter and flour, gradually add milk to create a béchamel sauce.
3. Stir in cheese until melted, season with salt and pepper.
4. Toss with conchiglie and serve hot.

Trofie al Pesto di Pistacchio

Ingredients:

- 400g trofie pasta
- 150g pistachios, shelled and unsalted
- 50g grated Parmesan
- 1 garlic clove
- 100ml olive oil
- Fresh basil leaves
- Salt and pepper to taste

Instructions:

1. Cook trofie in salted boiling water until al dente.
2. Blend pistachios, Parmesan, garlic, basil, and olive oil into a pesto.
3. Toss trofie with the pesto and serve.

Tagliatelle ai Carciofi

Ingredients:

- 400g tagliatelle pasta
- 4 artichokes, cleaned and sliced
- 2 garlic cloves, minced
- Olive oil
- 100ml white wine
- Fresh parsley, chopped
- Salt and pepper to taste
- Grated Parmesan for serving

Instructions:

1. Cook tagliatelle in salted boiling water until al dente.
2. Sauté garlic in olive oil, add artichokes, and cook until tender.
3. Deglaze with white wine, season with salt and pepper.
4. Toss tagliatelle with the artichokes, sprinkle with parsley, and serve with Parmesan.

Pappardelle al Cinghiale

Ingredients:

- 400g pappardelle pasta
- 500g wild boar, diced
- 1 onion, chopped
- 2 carrots, chopped
- 2 celery stalks, chopped
- 400g canned tomatoes
- 200ml red wine
- Olive oil
- Salt and pepper to taste
- Grated Parmesan for serving

Instructions:

1. Marinate wild boar in red wine overnight.
2. Sauté onion, carrots, and celery in olive oil, add the boar, and brown.
3. Add tomatoes, season with salt and pepper, and simmer until tender.
4. Cook pappardelle in salted water until al dente, then toss with the sauce.
5. Serve with Parmesan.

Penne Zucchine e Gamberetti

Ingredients:

- 400g penne pasta
- 2 zucchinis, sliced
- 300g shrimp, peeled and deveined
- 2 garlic cloves, minced
- Olive oil
- 100ml white wine
- Salt and pepper to taste
- Fresh parsley, chopped

Instructions:

1. Cook penne in salted boiling water until al dente.
2. Sauté garlic in olive oil, add zucchini and shrimp, and cook until shrimp is pink.
3. Deglaze with white wine, season with salt and pepper.
4. Toss penne with the shrimp and zucchini mixture, garnish with parsley, and serve.

Gnocchi di Patate al Tartufo

Ingredients:

- 500g potato gnocchi
- 40g black truffle, finely shaved
- 100g butter
- Salt to taste
- Grated Parmesan for serving

Instructions:

1. Cook gnocchi in salted boiling water until they float.
2. Melt butter in a skillet, add truffle shavings, and gently warm.
3. Toss gnocchi with the truffle butter and serve with Parmesan.

Pasta alla Genovese

Ingredients:

- 400g pasta (penne or ziti)
- 2 onions, thinly sliced
- 500g beef chuck, diced
- 100ml white wine
- Olive oil
- Salt and pepper to taste
- Grated Parmesan for serving

Instructions:

1. Sauté onions in olive oil until caramelized, add beef, and brown.
2. Deglaze with white wine, season with salt and pepper, and simmer until beef is tender.
3. Cook pasta in salted water until al dente, then toss with the sauce.
4. Serve with Parmesan.

Spaghetti alla Marinara

Ingredients:

- 400g spaghetti
- 400g canned tomatoes
- 2 garlic cloves, minced
- Olive oil
- Fresh basil leaves
- Salt to taste

Instructions:

1. Cook spaghetti in salted boiling water until al dente.
2. Sauté garlic in olive oil, add tomatoes, and simmer until sauce thickens.
3. Toss spaghetti with the sauce, garnish with basil, and serve.

Linguine alle Cozze

Ingredients:

- 400g linguine
- 1kg mussels, cleaned
- 2 garlic cloves, minced
- 100ml white wine
- Olive oil
- Fresh parsley, chopped
- Salt and pepper to taste

Instructions:

1. Cook linguine in salted boiling water until al dente.
2. Sauté garlic in olive oil, add mussels, and cook until they open.
3. Deglaze with white wine, season with salt and pepper.
4. Toss linguine with the mussels, sprinkle with parsley, and serve.

Maccheroni al Forno

Ingredients:

- 400g macaroni pasta
- 500ml béchamel sauce
- 200g mozzarella, diced
- 100g Parmesan, grated
- 100g cooked ham, diced
- Salt and pepper to taste

Instructions:

1. Cook macaroni in salted boiling water until al dente.
2. Mix macaroni with béchamel, mozzarella, ham, and half the Parmesan.
3. Transfer to a baking dish, top with remaining Parmesan, and bake at 180°C (350°F) until golden.

Penne alla Crudaiola

Ingredients:

- 400g penne pasta
- 4 ripe tomatoes, diced
- 2 garlic cloves, minced
- 100g mozzarella, diced
- Olive oil
- Fresh basil leaves
- Salt and pepper to taste

Instructions:

1. Cook penne in salted boiling water until al dente.
2. In a bowl, mix tomatoes, garlic, mozzarella, olive oil, basil, salt, and pepper.
3. Toss penne with the tomato mixture and serve.

Fusilli al Tonno

Ingredients:

- 400g fusilli pasta
- 200g canned tuna, drained
- 400g canned tomatoes
- 2 garlic cloves, minced
- Olive oil
- Salt and pepper to taste
- Fresh parsley, chopped

Instructions:

1. Cook fusilli in salted boiling water until al dente.
2. Sauté garlic in olive oil, add tomatoes and tuna, and cook until sauce thickens.
3. Toss fusilli with the sauce, sprinkle with parsley, and serve.

Paccheri con Melanzane e Ricotta

Ingredients:

- 400g paccheri pasta
- 2 large eggplants, diced
- 250g ricotta cheese
- 2 garlic cloves, minced
- Olive oil
- Fresh basil leaves
- Salt and pepper to taste
- Grated Parmesan for serving

Instructions:

1. Cook paccheri in salted boiling water until al dente.
2. Sauté garlic in olive oil, add eggplant, and cook until soft.
3. Mix ricotta with basil, salt, and pepper.
4. Toss paccheri with the eggplant and ricotta mixture.
5. Serve with grated Parmesan.

Pici all'Aglione

Ingredients:

- 400g pici pasta
- 6 garlic cloves, minced
- 400g canned tomatoes
- Olive oil
- Salt and pepper to taste
- Fresh parsley, chopped

Instructions:

1. Cook pici in salted boiling water until al dente.
2. Sauté garlic in olive oil until golden.
3. Add tomatoes, season with salt and pepper, and simmer until sauce thickens.
4. Toss pici with the sauce, sprinkle with parsley, and serve.

Tortelloni di Zucca

Ingredients:

- 400g tortelloni filled with pumpkin
- 100g butter
- 6 sage leaves
- Salt and pepper to taste
- Grated Parmesan for serving

Instructions:

1. Cook tortelloni in salted boiling water until al dente.
2. Melt butter in a skillet, add sage leaves, and cook until fragrant.
3. Toss tortelloni with the sage butter and serve with Parmesan.

Strozzapreti al Ragù di Coniglio

Ingredients:

- 400g strozzapreti pasta
- 500g rabbit meat, diced
- 1 onion, chopped
- 2 carrots, chopped
- 2 celery stalks, chopped
- 200ml white wine
- 400g canned tomatoes
- Olive oil
- Salt and pepper to taste

Instructions:

1. Sauté onion, carrots, and celery in olive oil.
2. Add rabbit, brown, then deglaze with white wine.
3. Add tomatoes, season with salt and pepper, and simmer until tender.
4. Cook strozzapreti in salted water until al dente, then toss with the ragù and serve.

Orecchiette al Pomodoro e Basilico

Ingredients:

- 400g orecchiette pasta
- 400g canned tomatoes
- 2 garlic cloves, minced
- Olive oil
- Fresh basil leaves
- Salt and pepper to taste
- Grated Parmesan for serving

Instructions:

1. Cook orecchiette in salted boiling water until al dente.
2. Sauté garlic in olive oil, add tomatoes, and simmer until sauce thickens.
3. Toss orecchiette with the sauce, garnish with basil, and serve with Parmesan.

Fregola con Vongole

Ingredients:

- 400g fregola pasta
- 1kg clams, cleaned
- 2 garlic cloves, minced
- 100ml white wine
- Olive oil
- Fresh parsley, chopped
- Salt and pepper to taste

Instructions:

1. Cook fregola in salted boiling water until al dente.
2. Sauté garlic in olive oil, add clams, and cook until they open.
3. Deglaze with white wine, season with salt and pepper.
4. Toss fregola with the clams, sprinkle with parsley, and serve.

Ravioli al Tartufo

Ingredients:

- 400g ravioli filled with truffle
- 100g butter
- 40g black truffle, finely shaved
- Salt to taste
- Grated Parmesan for serving

Instructions:

1. Cook ravioli in salted boiling water until al dente.
2. Melt butter in a skillet, add truffle shavings, and gently warm.
3. Toss ravioli with the truffle butter and serve with Parmesan.

Spaghetti con Bottarga

Ingredients:

- 400g spaghetti
- 50g bottarga, grated
- 2 garlic cloves, minced
- Olive oil
- Fresh parsley, chopped
- Salt to taste

Instructions:

1. Cook spaghetti in salted boiling water until al dente.
2. Sauté garlic in olive oil, then add half the bottarga.
3. Toss spaghetti with the bottarga mixture, sprinkle with remaining bottarga and parsley, and serve.

www.ingramcontent.com/pod-product-compliance
Lightning Source LLC
LaVergne TN
LVHW081324060526
838201LV00055B/2447